Igloo Press, Tucson, Arizona
www.igloopress.net

ISBN 978-0-9787608-2-3

For information, write:
Igloo Press
2940 16th St. Suite 216,
San Francisco, CA 94103.

Hold Still Please

Poetry by
Tina Huerta

Photography
by Will Turner

For Bob

For Sue

TOC

tina
1997

APPRECIATION

Dashing men
have a sworn secret
& I am one.

Whispering encouragements
protecting what they themselves might destroy
nudging smiles
wrestling away the wounds
bandaging the guilt
patient of their beastful brethren.

Dashing men
with noble insight
to culture breath
have a fellow accomplice
& I am one.

Accompanying me
the floundering child of promise
holding out strength
a finger to my clutching
reach of independence
a beauty for all listening quietly
resting against the din.

Dashing men
cautious of placement
when the curtain parts
Directors relaxing
lucidity of flight
intimate with each stroke
& I am one.

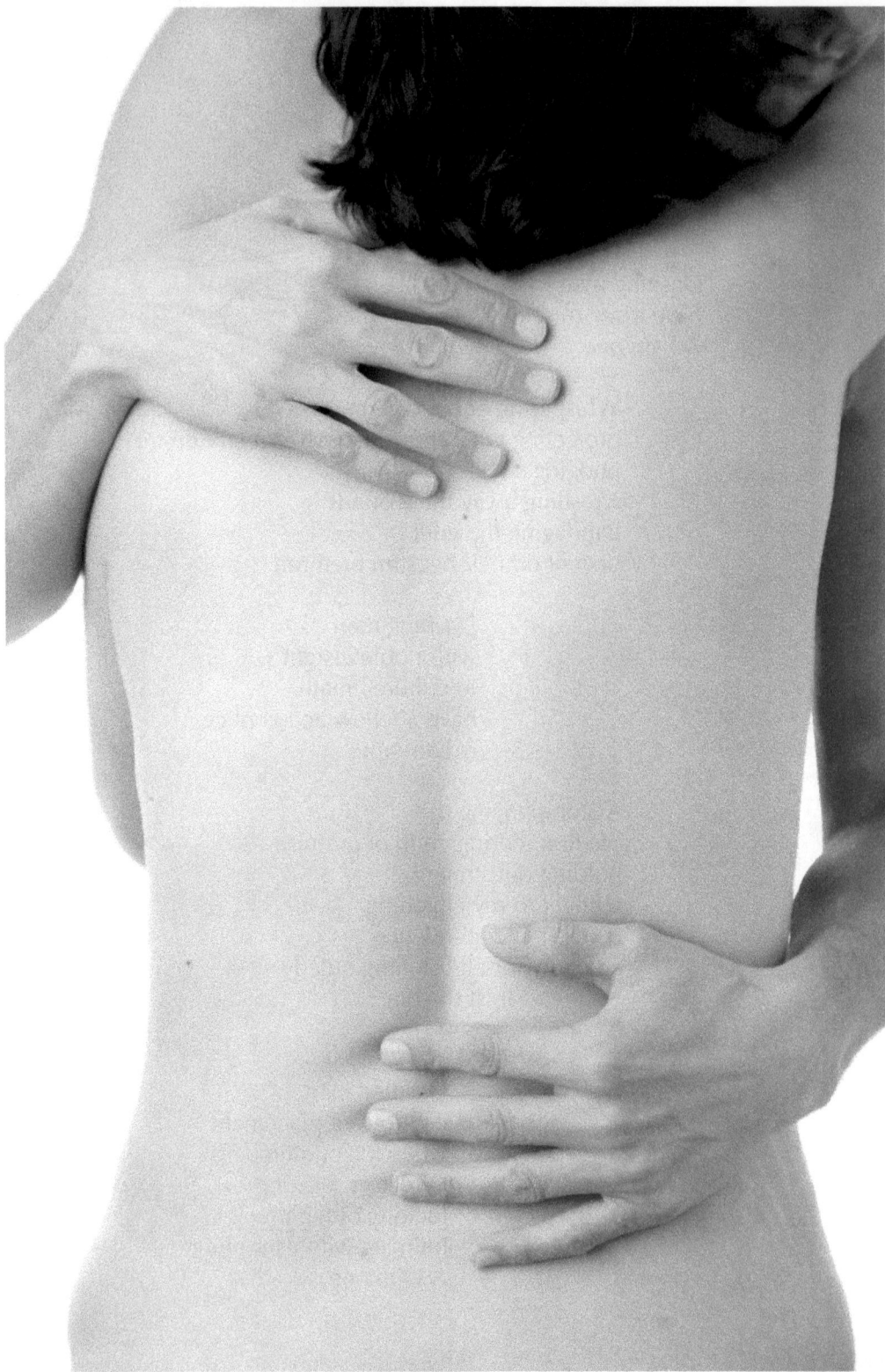

tina
1998

SACRIFICE

How dare I try to compete
with your beloved past love lost.
You just wanted comfort
and I tried to give you so much more.

How dare I try to impress you
with what I have to offer,
You must feel guilt
feeling you have nothing
left to offer.

Sunshine,
you're in no shape
to shine just yet.
Let your head set
in my lap
and let your heart go
as far thru the pain
and the joy
of your lost love.
Gain back that love
cause it's yours
and hers.
You'll need that to go on.

I'm here to hold you
till you shine once more.
It would be futile to touch
the sun.
But the sun shines
for everyone
as long as it shines.

tina
2000

SO THERE

You shook your head
            laughing
    in between
        saying good-byes
            and friends waiting in line
waiting for their kiss good-bye
        from them
            to me
                to you.

I never waited for you
    yet you came
    keeping a ten-year promise.

That love will always be kept
            beneath the laughter
across your top lip.
    Tucked inside our hearts
        replenishing our paths
to cross forever in our minds.

You never let me
    forget that I am a woman
You never questioned my desires
        reassuring your presence
            every escort
    holding every lasting moment
                precious
sequestering my attention
            to your attentiveness
        your unrelenting patience…

I cried watching you
    running aside that train
        ten years for good-bye
        drenched in moonlight.

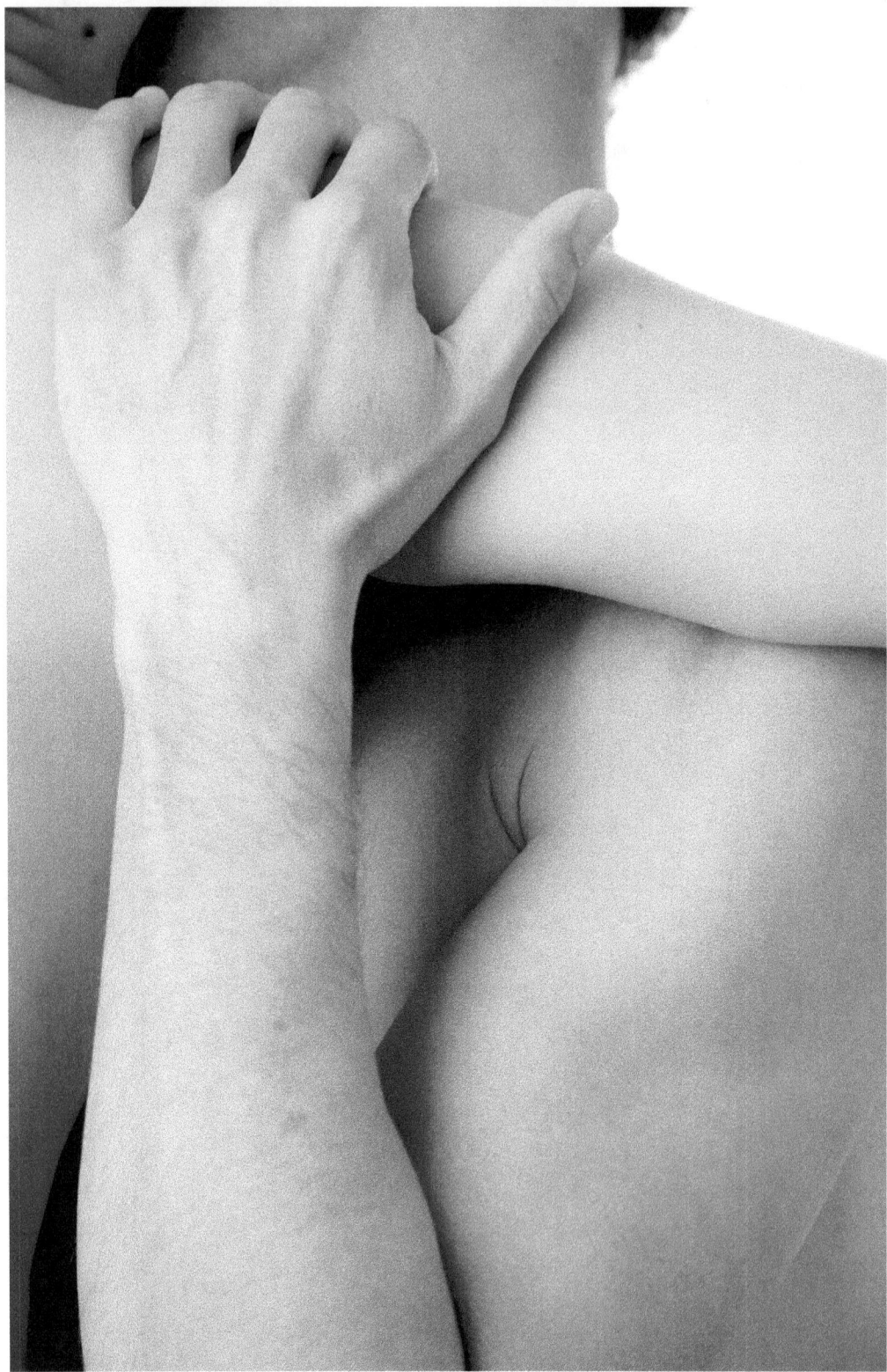

tina
1989

TW

I admired his movement
in the mirror behind the bar.
"I just got out of jail."
Wow. What a first line!

I wondered
as his statement
whisped through his
lollipop face,
lemondrop dimples,
melted buttered hair,
and impish lips.
Must have been
a stupid law.

He gathered me up
in his whirlwind visit
to this dusty town,
I left him sleeping
undisturbed to my
morning schedule.

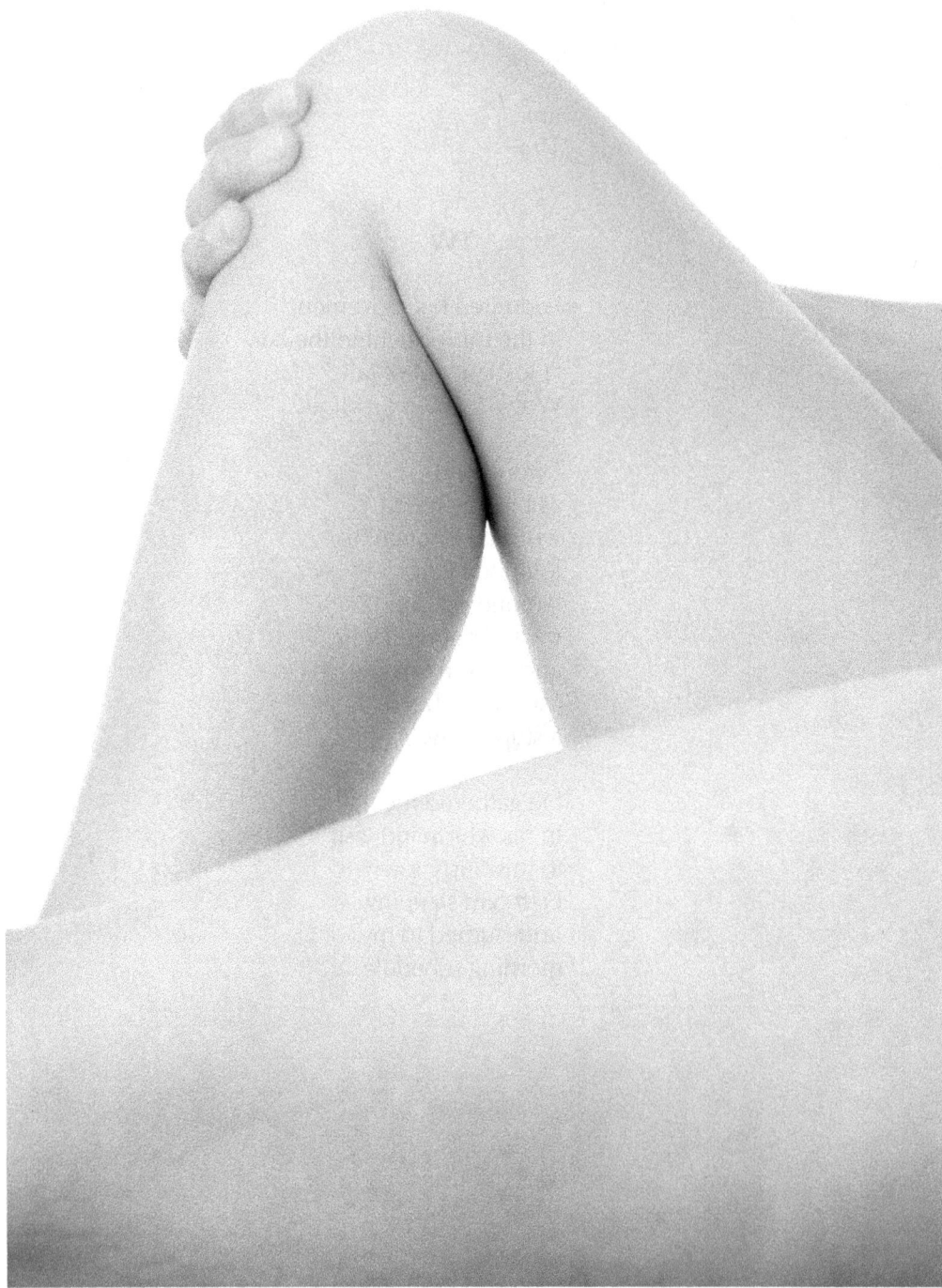

tina
2001

THE CAPE

Nothing
right now
could make me happier
than the thought
of you
appearing out of nowhere
in pursuit of me.

You and your blue eyes
and that dark hair
lightly seasoned in white

I knew you would smile
as soon as I saw you
Do you take a deep breath as well
then toss out the rest of the world
like the matador
with his cape?

How I wish you would appear
out of nowhere
that would be too easy
I'll have to face my fear
and drive up that long driveway
Men wait too long
brush aside women of mixed signals

What do they call that –
low self-esteem.
only to produce that motion
repeated   brushing aside
'til it's forgotten
not this time
I will be brave
my breath to be taken
driving up that long driveway.

tina
1989

WITHIN YOUR GRASP

I stand in the epicenter
a shuttle terminal
sweaty grimy from months past
depositing insurgent supplies
to allied posts
in thick frontier planets.

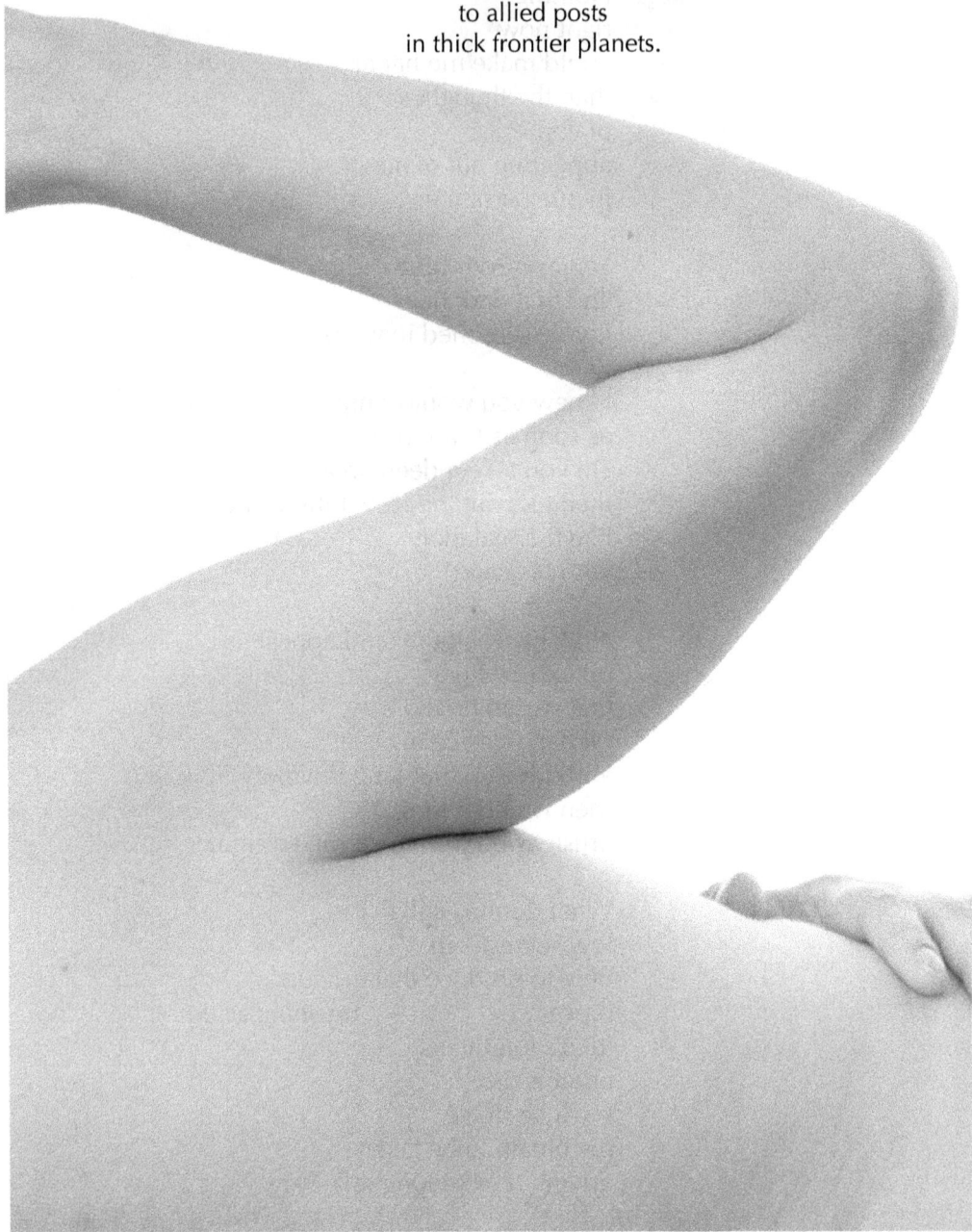

I access my pocket computer
for random departure listings
searching for the next flight
to port Space Station Cirrus.
Exhausted by both
physical and mental exercises
effectively coping foreign terrains
monitoring non-linear communications
a haunting ad rings
cutting away the shuffling scene
vacationers and preoccupied scientists
pulsing to the heartbeat
of my info screen.

It whispers an obscure   ancient name -
"Yahad."
I board the hissing transport
sizing-up sometimes suspecting passengers
ready to battle possible future Virgil ventures
planted within sight
of plated strands of sticky hair
never loosening my grip
of a prepaid ticket
carrying the name "Yahad."

unwittingly I've been assigned
navigator honorarium
meta silk spinning
moon child of Yahad
A pensive drifting flight
expulsing insecurity of faith
soaring shards of light -

The warm wet sand
presses caressingly 'neath my frightened face
fresh tears bathe the shallows of my eyes
willfully spilling
finally absolving
into the bleached sand pearls
within your smile
whispering the name   "Yahad."

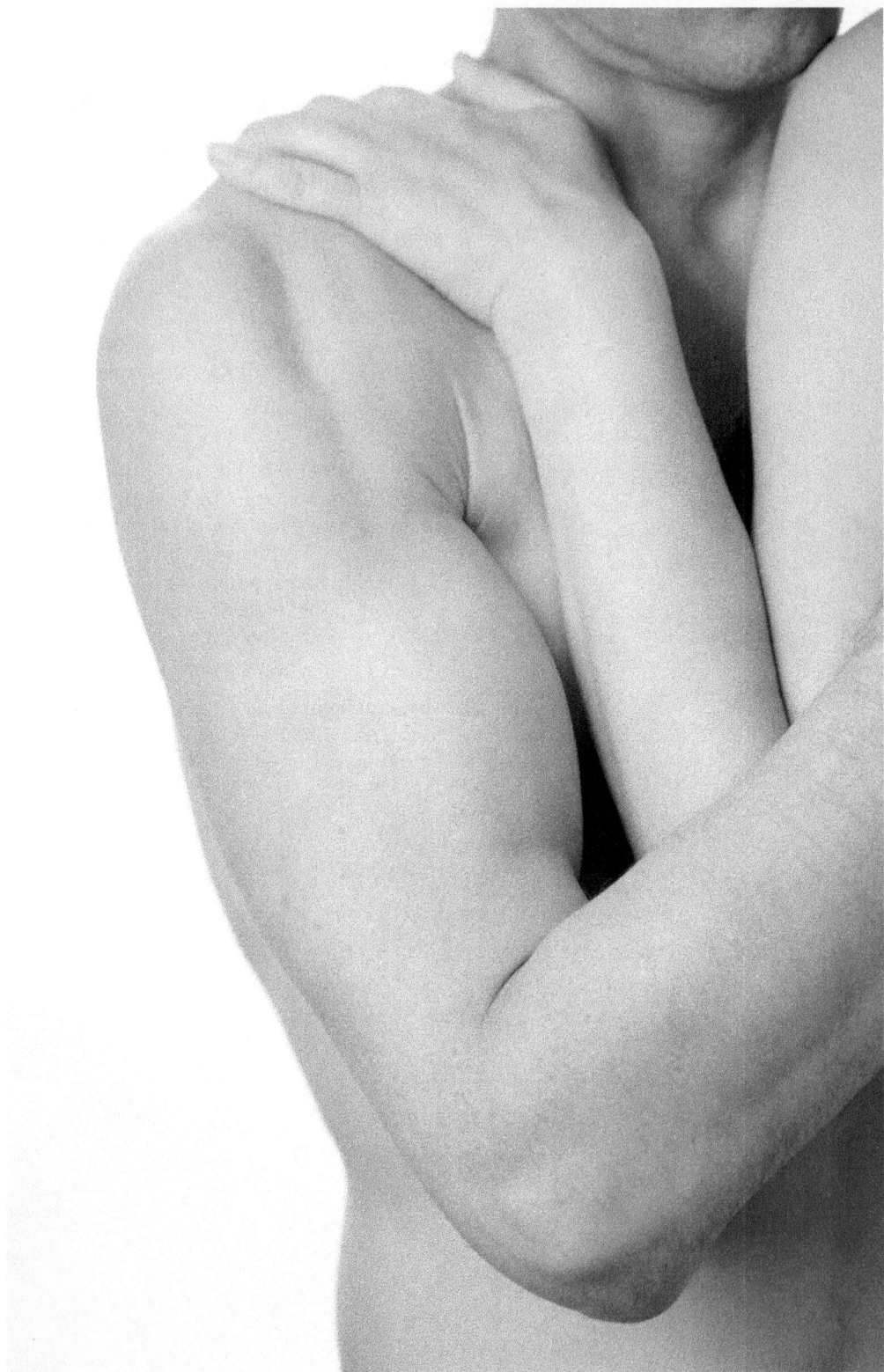

FINDING MR.GOODBAR

Crazy Vato.
>   Six-foot, white skin, blue-eyed Fem
>   slinging his bokken.
>   Only thing stopping a Blood or Crypt in his tracks
>   is that righteous black beret.

Crazy Vato.
>   Reading 500 words per minute
>   while I'm still stuck on the first page.
>   What do you mean -
>   Tucson's not a cow-town
>   unless you define the cows as tourists?
>   Wish I had a whiplash tongue.

Crazy Vato.
>   Creamy skin, long slender extremities
>   Hips that rotate to guitars
>   not drums
>   Restricted only by bodies
>   and walls
>   His dance demands a stage
>   his heart an audience.

Crazy Vato.
>   Wants a black gerbil -   fuck a cage
>   we gotta house.
>   You wanna make milk carton airplanes
>   with GI Joes parachuting out
>   rescuing Barbie from the burning doll house
>   in the hallway?
>   God I'm in love!

Crazy Vato.
>   Yeah the world is fucked
>   and children are dying.
>   They wouldn't know an offering
>   or an answer
>   if it came with credit card approval.

Crazy Vato.
>   What do you mean
>   --baggy pants--
>   you're a vato?
>   --skinny undershirt--
>   You have
>   --black trench coat--
>   fuchsia hair and
>   --blue bandanna--
>   freckles ?
>   --cool shades-- --haughty smile--

>   "You know   mannn...- -   --Vaato."

tina
1998

PORTAL

I've stripped to my bones
  skeleton walking
It's called the pain of flesh
  the flesh that holds
  the memories
    the sweet heartache.

I walk my halls
  alone forever this night
wind flowing thru
  empty doorways
  and thinly dressed windows
quietly murmuring your ghost
    our past
  searching for a glimpse
  of your heroic return.

I rummage thru the treasure box
sometimes sitting inside
  finding strands of your hair
  pieces of your laughter
wrapped in your reassurance
washing thru the tears
seeping thru my bones.

  At the core
my bones hold not the least
  bit of value
  to your heart.
All the treasure in this box
is mine alone.

My waiting may be wasteful
distasteful to your mind
  yet this place will stay
entombed as not so living art
  marking a karmic threshold
  lessons hardest learned
not so easily divulged
  of unconditional love.

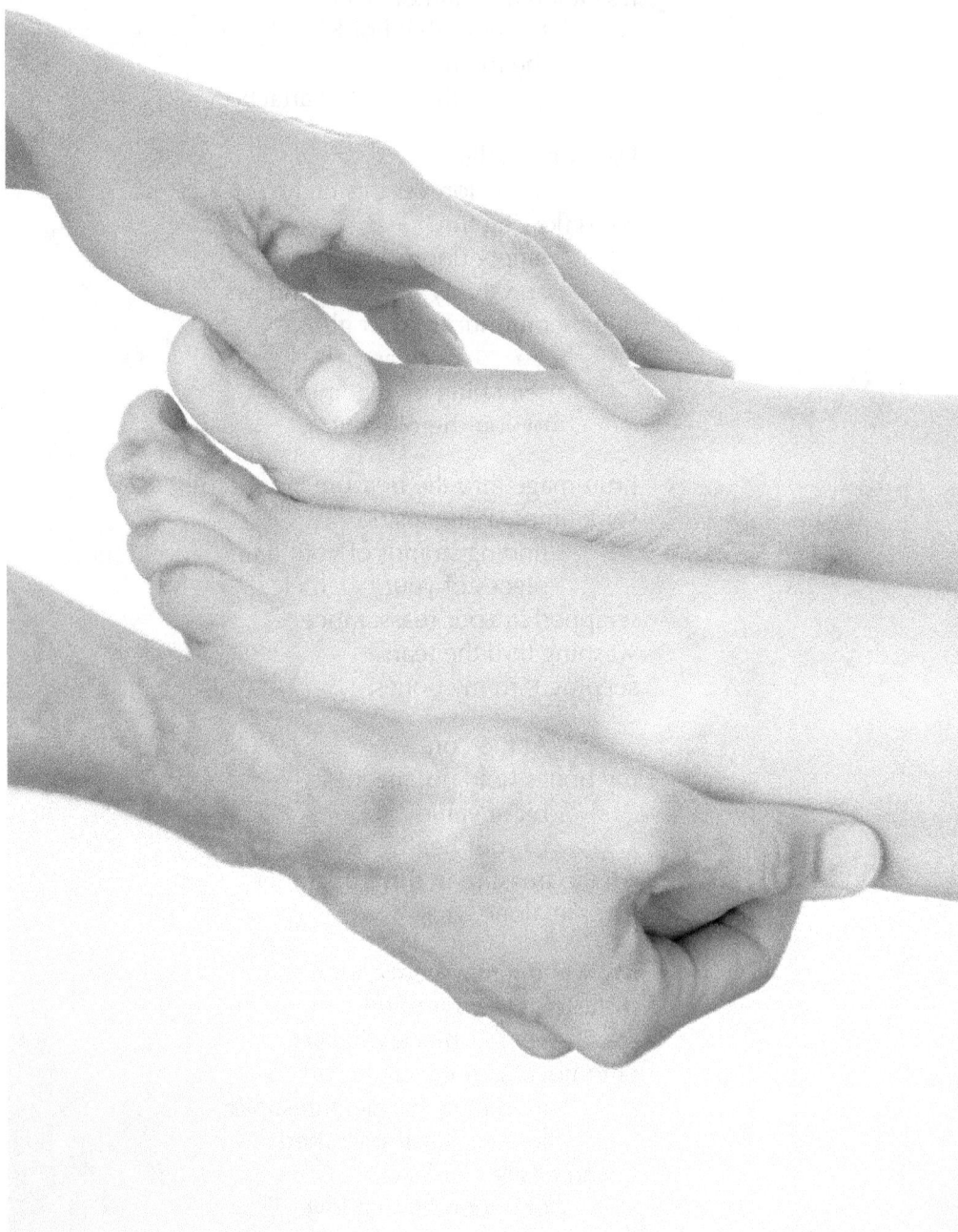

tina
2002

STRIP POKER

"Uh yeah, this is tina."
Why do I sound so stupid?
Even my voice cracks.
    Nervous? – yes.
Scared I'll blow it.

Should I pretend it's not you?
What happened to my sense of humor?
    I wish it had left me naked,
clown shoes by themselves
make it hard to recover
    any sense of dignity
what-so-ever.

I promise next-time
to start with a glass of wine
    at least I'm cute
    when I'm drunk
Gay Bradley said so.
If you were gay Bradley
    you would tell me to
"Just shut-up and relax."
Of course, he would giggle first.

    I apologize.
My messages have been so lame
Even on stage
    the stand-by terror
never stops the performance.
I just let go
    and release my heart.

But an audience guarantees gratitude
    to well spoken talent
especially those gracious exhibitionists.

Tell me
you have some trepidation
And your self-confidence
    Just a silly shield.

tina
1995

SOUL TWIN

I've lost the will to stay afloat
constantly above each wave.

I accept the overwash of each wave
Knowing I can take breath on the next.

Security and comfort of presence
the light is strong and permeates
both salt and each motion.

The sea is no longer fearful
no longer alien
no longer desperate.
The sea and I are one
turning and diving the sea mammal I am.

My world has become a dream
as I go thru this sea.

A dream of long ago
a staircase dissension
into a clear shallow sea
a sunlit swim cleansing my soul
taking me far out to the open sea
Struggling a private barrier
and disappointment of retreat
holding onto realization of future
longing the deep dear sea.

This dream of long ago.
Has become more than just a dream.

this is my dream
my dream of safety
my dream of peace
my dream of hope
time has no presence.
there is no cold
within warmth
within protection
within permanence
place has no distance.

New dreams begin
        laughter is here
                        tears rejoice
                                        comfort is sought
                        gained
                                I sweep the universe
delightful of freedom
        of ecstasy   of myself   within   throughout.

        Places I have wandered
        anxious to share
        treasures of the mind
        sun driven cloud rides,
        rain patter forest canopies,
        un mundo para yos corozones solas,
        conventions of like souls
        exchanging gifts,
        pleasures of flight,
        a few thousand years in training
        preparations for growth,
        emersion shifting atoms.
        this is what I feel
        in this ocean.
        An ocean of tsunamis
        doldrums
        icebergs
        warm beaches
        and living creatures within.
        It heaves and subsides
        as my blood shifts
        transmuting chemistry
        profusing endorphins
        keeping me on edge
        harboring
        at bay
        my emotions.

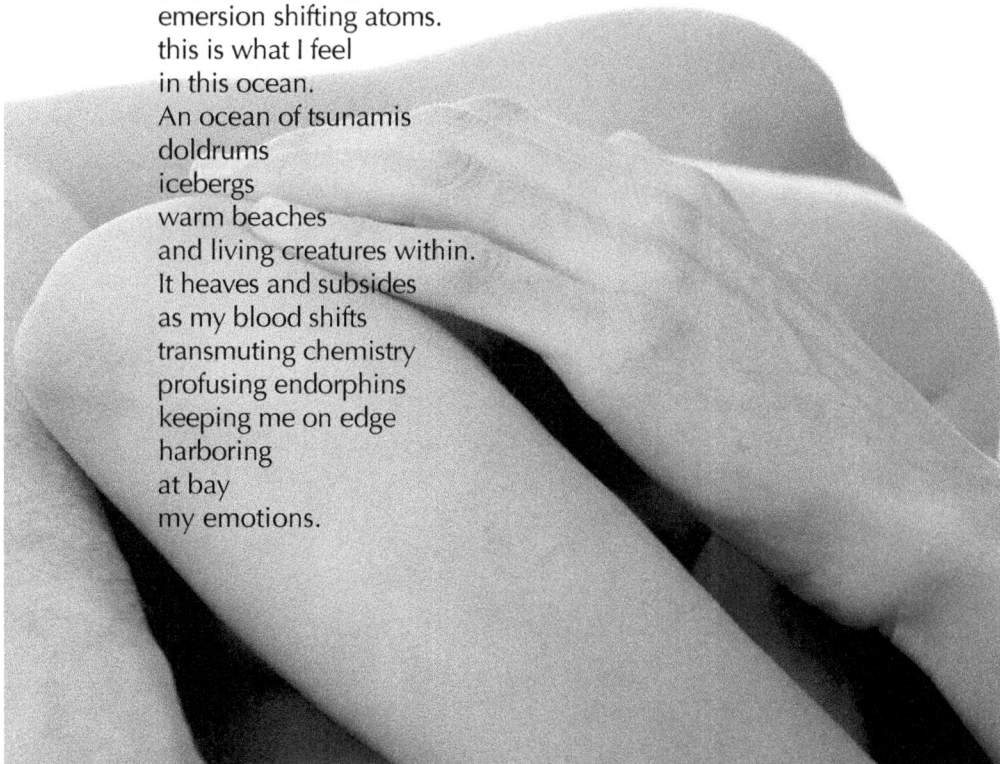

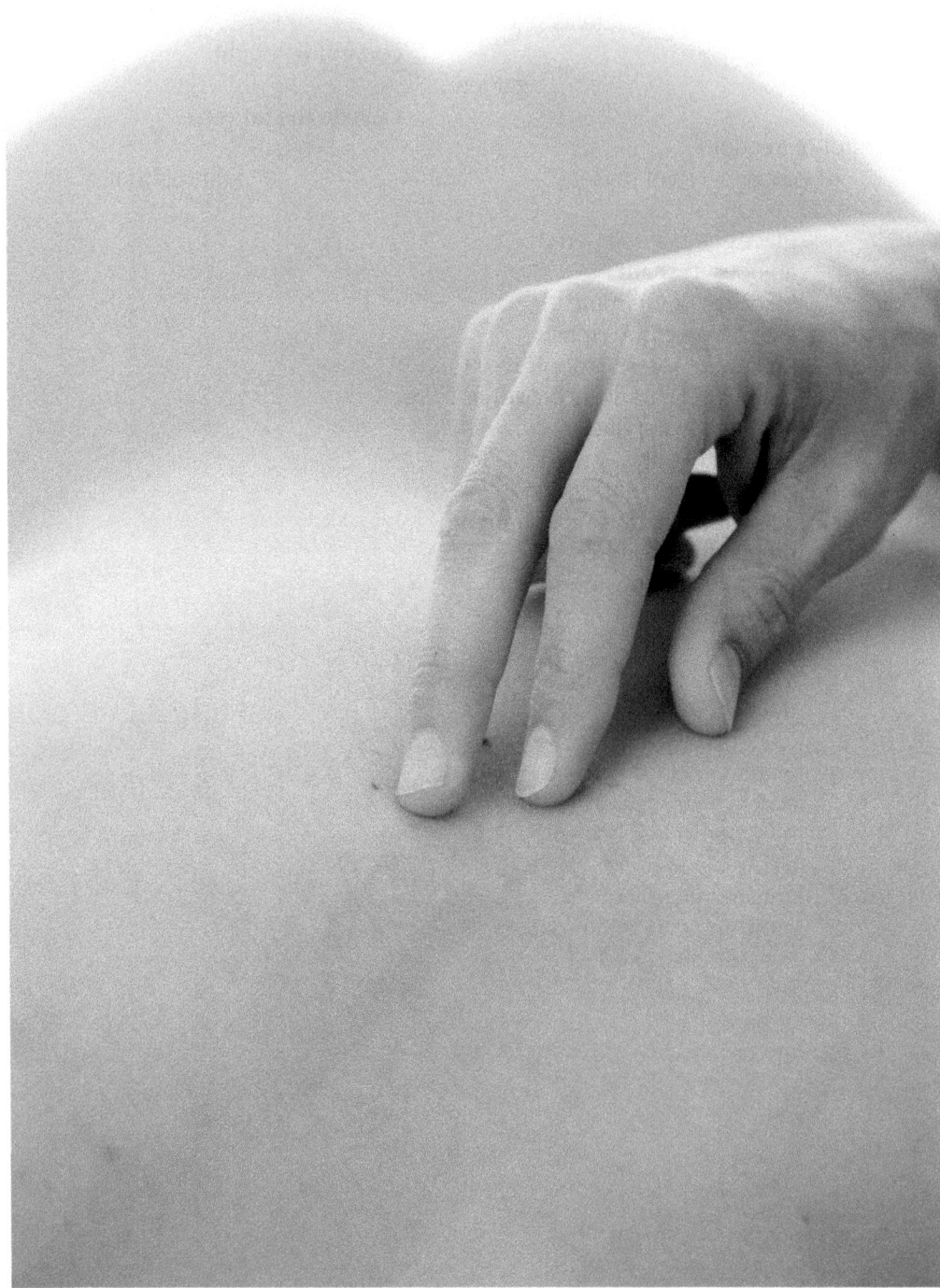

tina
1989

SCORPIO DELIGHT

He's such a puzzle.
I'm so intrigued,
I've become immersed
with his strategy.

He spent an hour
deciphering my
surreal poem
towing and yanking
his fervent brain.

He believes
as I do
participation is
one-hundred percent,
times players,
times anticipation.

Never neglecting
consideration of
entropy, randomness
and divine intervention.

Our world is spent
in crowded extremes
of complicated
mixed-up emotions.

And now I
ramble the day
pursuing and probing
his ambrosiac song.

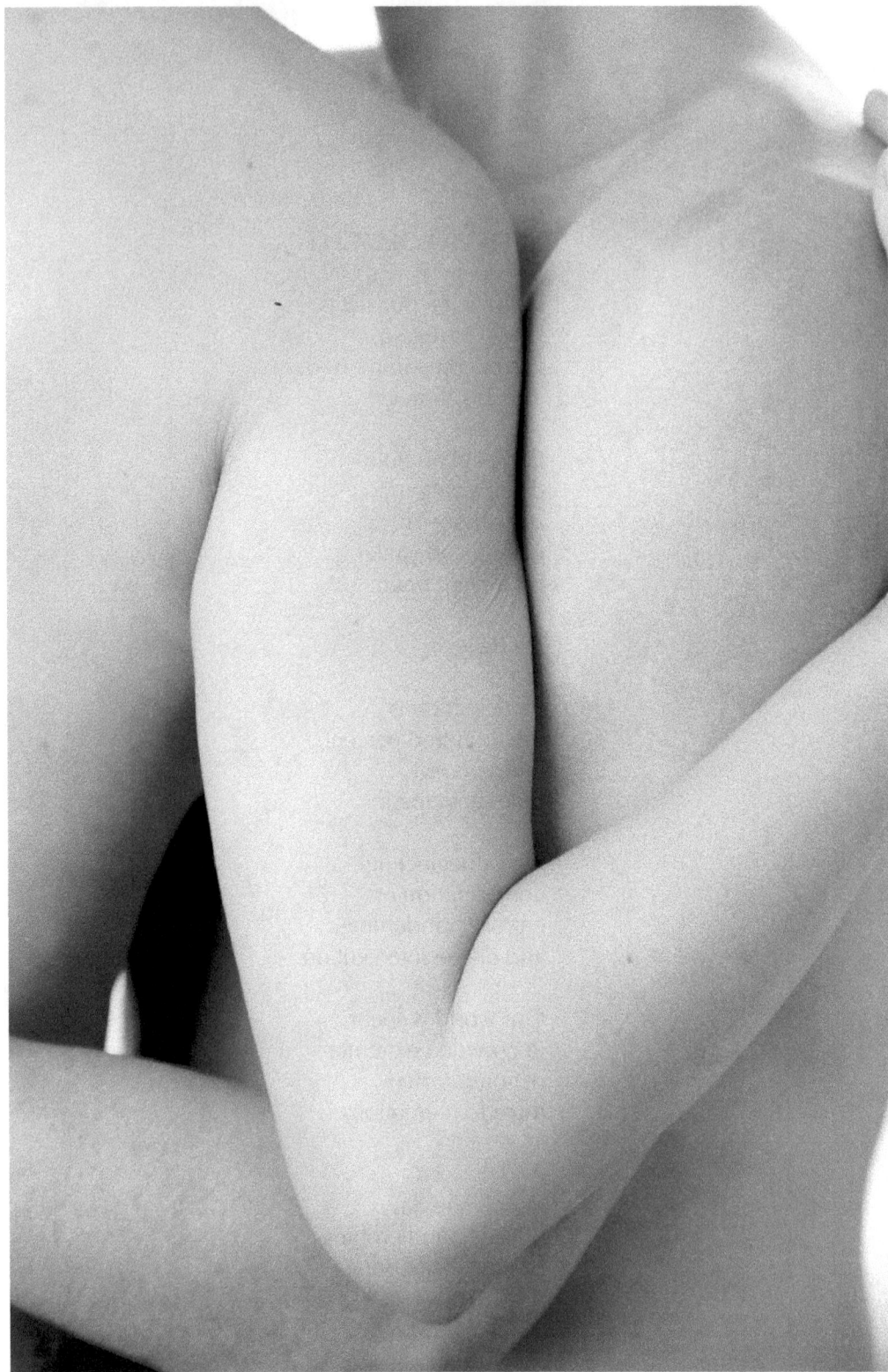

tina
2008

del SUBMAR-I-NER

I fall-float immersed
leagues beneath
You've opened a world
4 my mind play

the sub not silenced
amplifies the atmosphere
gliding wings with wind whispers
relaxing expansive
reaching muscles stretching
manic mind release

the universe echoes
against itself
repeating
time energy motion
energy motion time
release

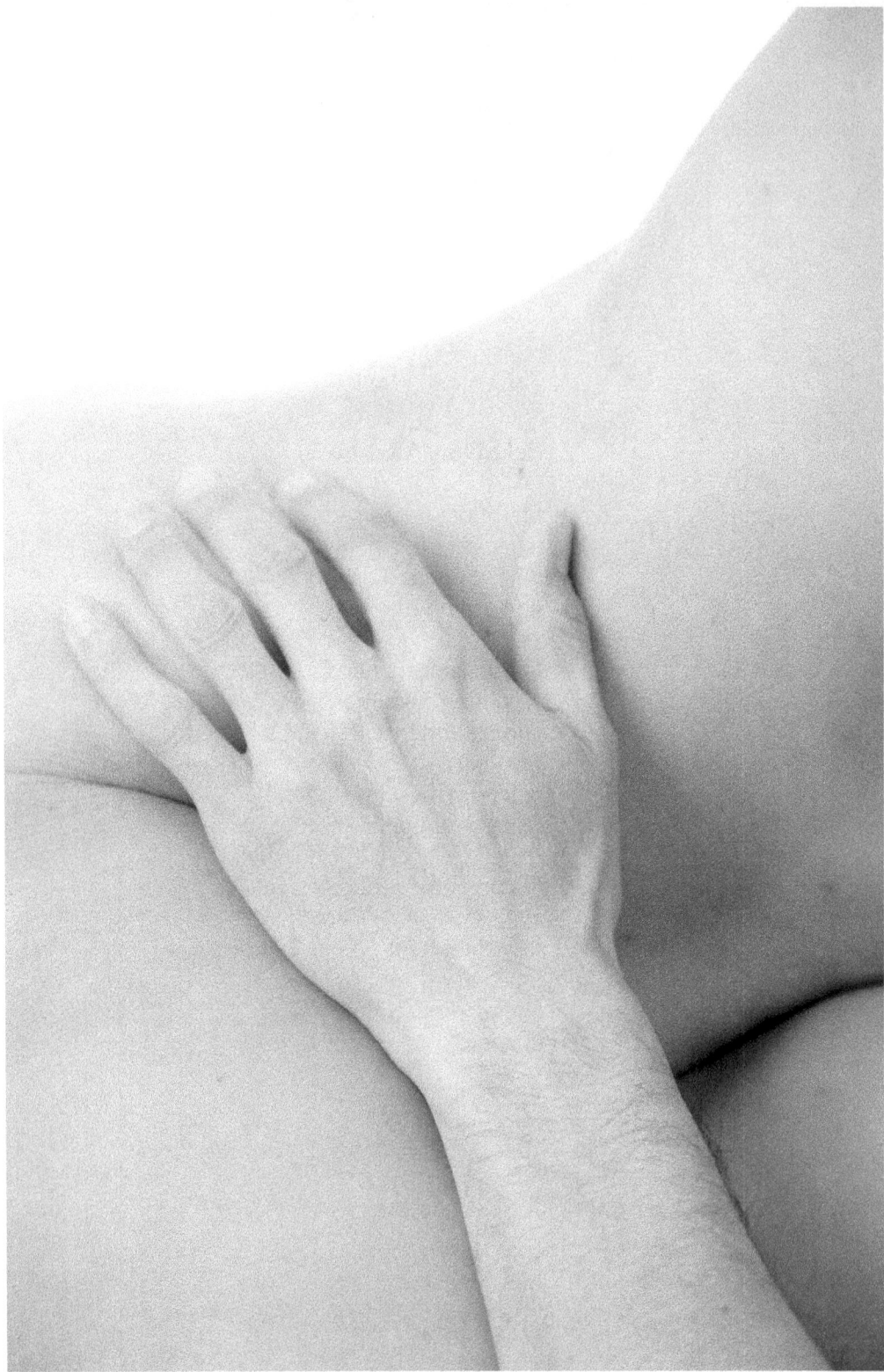

ETHEREAL REIN

Sprinkles of laughter
      other children fly by
smiles frozen in painted time.

Parents relinquishing restraints
      in a haven of painted booths
           displaying boisterous puppets
and dissolving cotton candy.

      The twirling movement
           of the statued carousel
                  draws me to its perimeter.
      Creatures in motionless movement
                expressing the tempo of boxed music.
          Animals with tall legs
             and shapely cropped wooden manes
           captured for their artistic shades.

      My eyes search each one
           for a beckoning sign
      of kicking and bounding life.
           The one in the middle swings by
     pressed for the galloping run.
          His clean sifted dusky mane
      stands back from his violet blue eyes
          his gently firmed body ready to ride.

I press my hands cautiously
          on his creamy glazed hind
and lift my body
        now fashioned in velvet hide.
     I raise and roll myself
       onto his custom made saddle
         clinging to the back of his neck
feeling the dew air rush by.

I open my eyes
    with comforting vision
        to see him rising
from my abdomen lagoon.
        His sighing awe
    captures my life stream breath
        and I lose my mind
to the continual circular stride.

META-MORPHOSIS

tina
1998

We've gorged ourselves historically
moving steadily underleaf
commonistically casually camouflaged,

drawing enough room for introspect
insuring natural survival
through invertedness.

Slowly gathering spun material
self-produced mantric fables

enhancing cosmic manifistic destiny
Building safe passage
and hopeful harmonic resolution

A fiber so strong
seducing song from slight air.
Light vibrates continuously within
filtered, gathered
absolution for our thirsts

Limbs reshape outer appearances
shifting molding movement
stretching our bodies within
gathering supple growth
encasing carnal supplication
welcoming universal dust

and possibilities of flight.

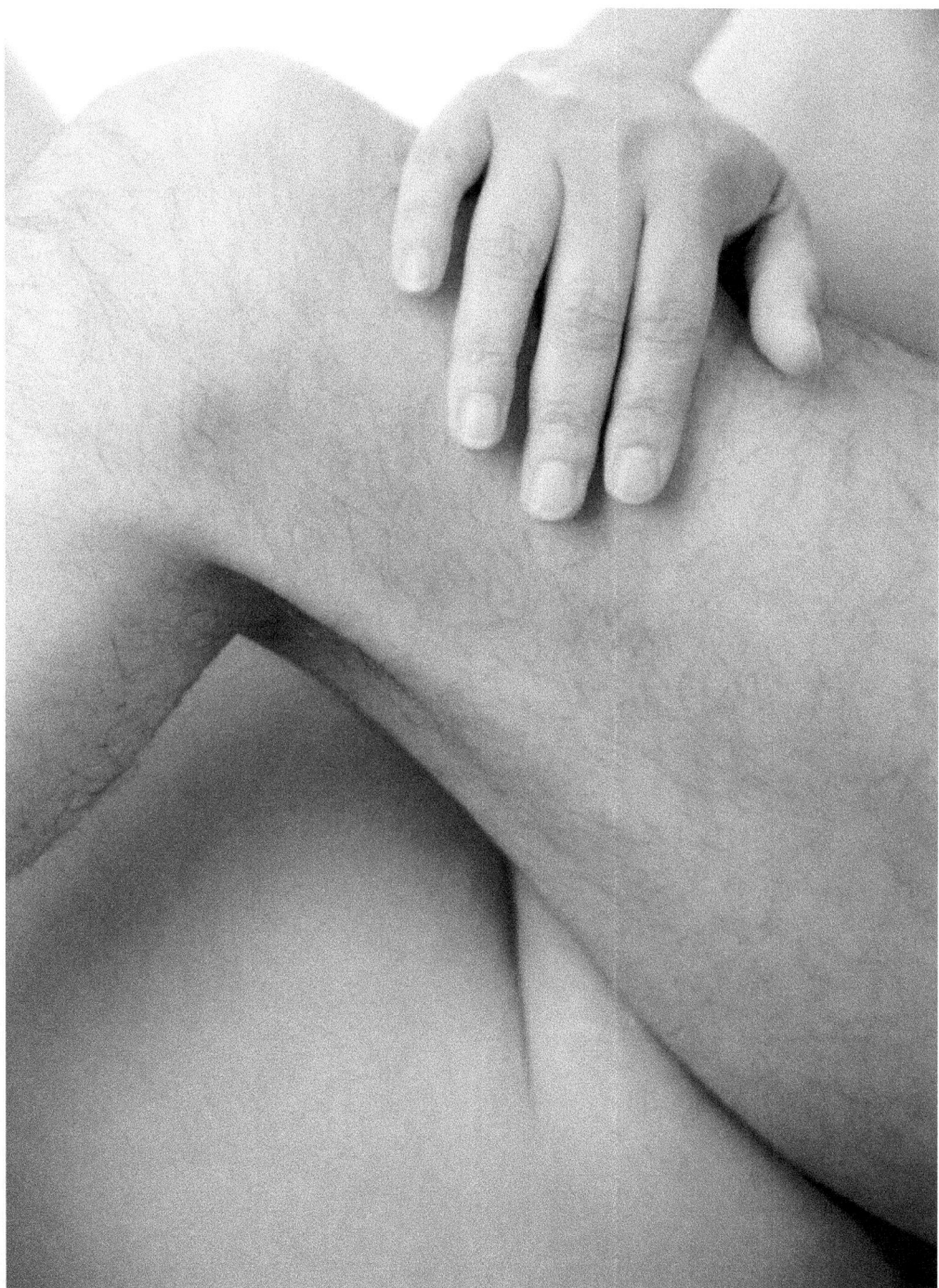

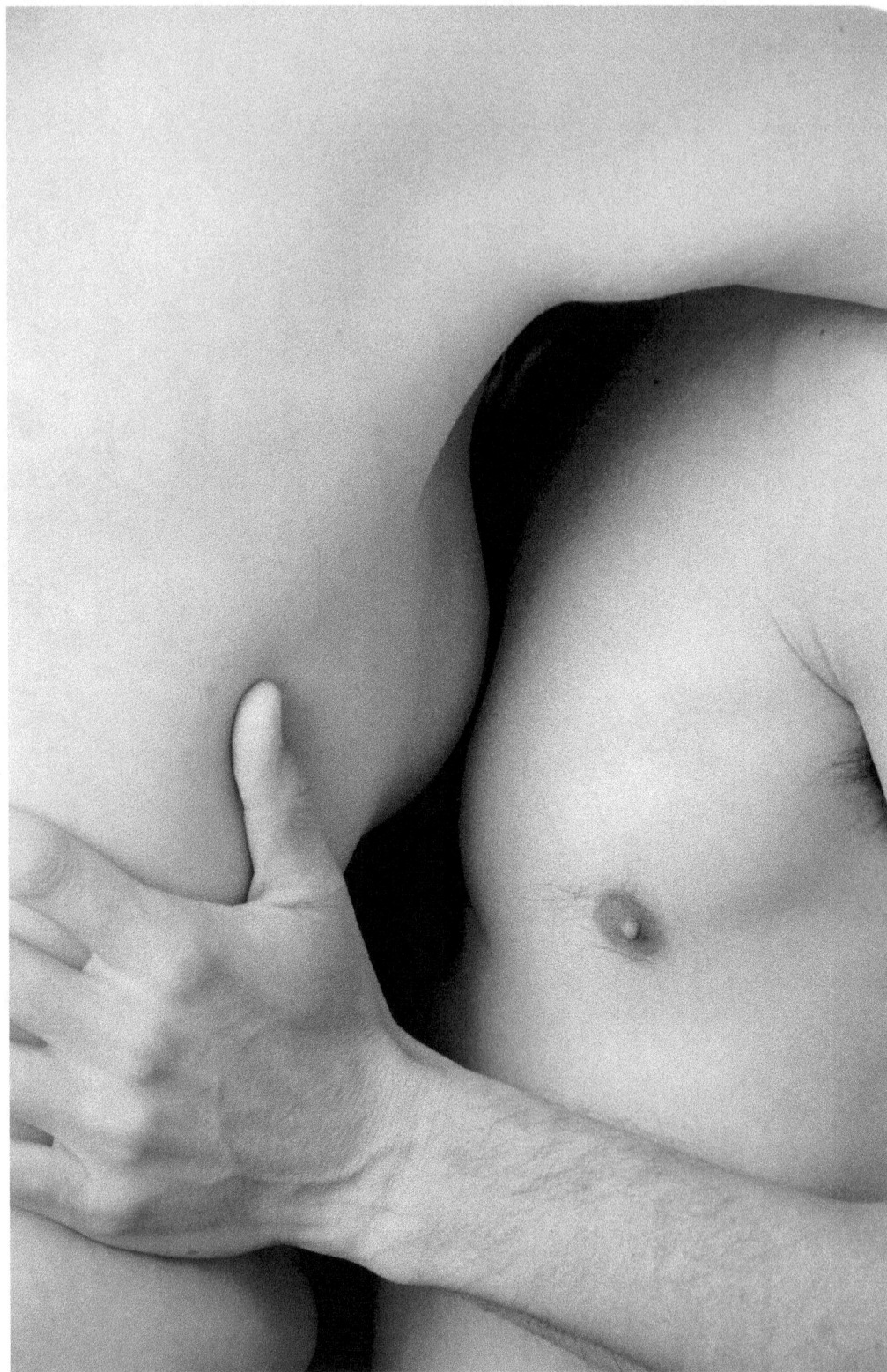

tina
2002

DAR

Coerced to watch
the passion of another poet
the master Rumi
            - altho exalted
sheds nothing new
The wind and the oceans do more.

For in each breath
  I feel you reaching
inside of me
      moving universes aside
    leaving room
            for our entwine
      stars pass thru
    what we bring together
shines fluorescently thru our veins
      our veins and cells
        infusing as one
          together.

Lingering the time
        suspended tapestry
          cell soul recognition
      integration of the mind
          a union cast
      long ago

  a gentle wisp
    summoning solid
        quantum connectivity

dismissing the urgency

  of here and now.

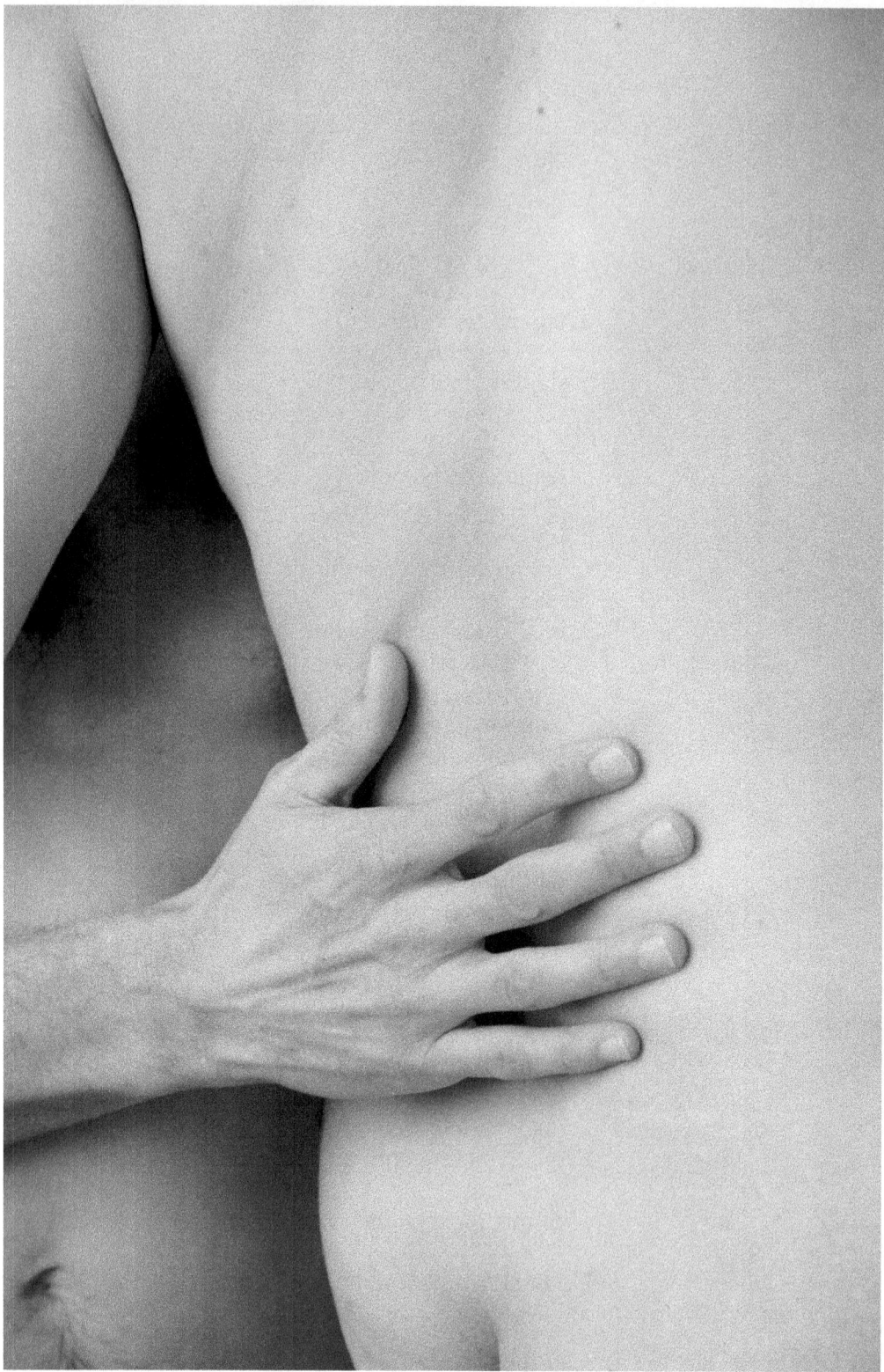

tina
2002

PROMENADE

                    Slipping thru
another dimension busy outside
            we celebrate
Glasses filled
time waits
out of mind,

Each breath
crashes down
  each moment
strong against our chests
each embrace
    tendered long
    birthed strong
rolling thru the sea
        as one.

 No hush or rustle
it's understood
the universe is set aside
  ever diligent
patient
        savoring each moment
      as we enjoin
tenderness and love.

CANOPY

This forest
most silent
the occasional branch break
underfoot
carrying the call
of your name
resonating
echoing against the emptiness

the journey
crushes the stride
step by steep step
up that mountain
alone

foot follows a forsaken path
os
Never to have been

the distant
Surf filling
Footprints still feeling
Sand grains and small pools
Eye salt melting with the tide
shifting movement of the earth
is felt
sliding this milky way
abandoning a bayful
resonance of soul

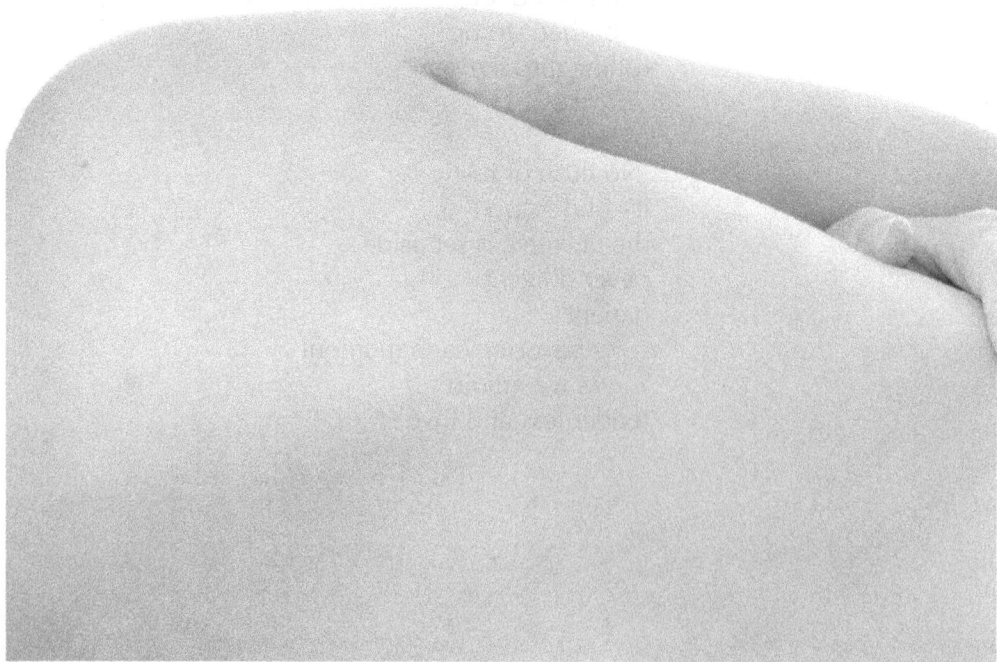

my mind resigns
the spirit recluse
the promise returned
honor unbequeathed
cast upon stars
and heaven untouched

I face this quiet breeze
the mountain trail
bristles bright
sparkle of sunshine
the air of nothingness
crisply cursing the soul
carrying the hope
of your name.

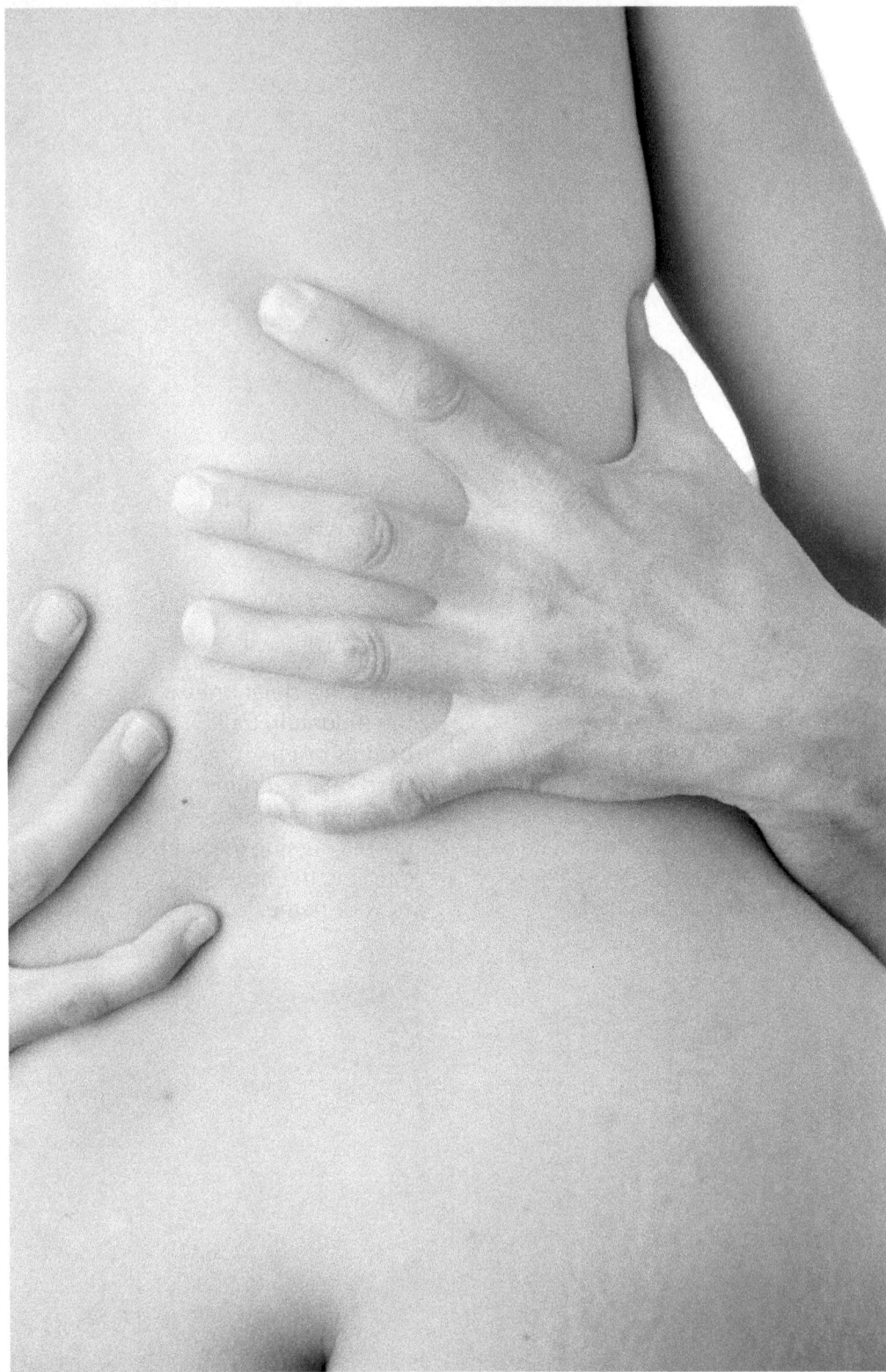

tina
1996

SUPPLE

And you
the stature
the presence
the softness
of poseidon
standing on the ocean floor,
allowing my flow
down your skin

within your mouth
within your essence
within your mind,
holding moments
movement

mirth.

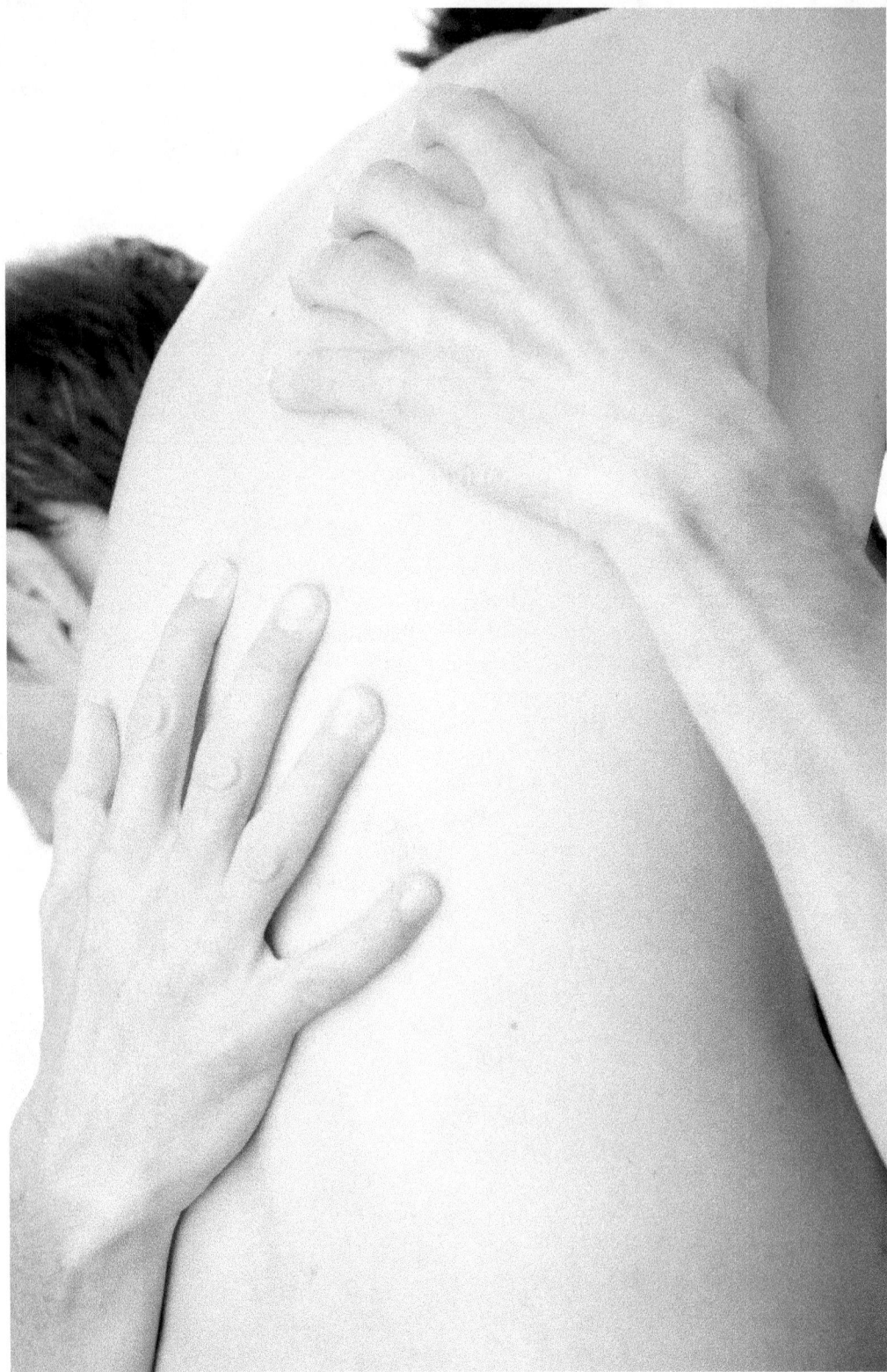

tina
1998

ALL OVER AGAIN

Tingling warm and wet
  the slide and closeness
Of total embrace.

That's mostly what I remember
buried under layers
buried under comforts
buried under pillows
Memories of my mother
  reopened by your arms.

Maybe it's your long dark hair
Maybe it's your smile
Maybe it's your touch
Your voice
 Your silence
  Your purpose
   Your height
     Your endurance
The strength of your legs.

But mostly
it's the loss
brought on by your absence.

tina
1990

DEBAUCHERY

Hopscotch squares it down the line,

     the line of what?

Broken pieces of white chalk

     leaving creamy powder

     within my palm.

How long was it?

     -eons of sunsets and marshmallows ago.

Somehow ending where it began

     somehow beginning where it ended

someone left a circle of footprints in the sand

     protecting me

       leaving me

         -stranding me

Praying I would walk away again.

tina
2000

2, 3, 4...

whispering
incredulous sexual revelation
how ridiculous!
Who ever heard of such a thing?
            - "the black queen of Barbarella"

the screen screaming
                    "angels have no memory"
definitions strewn
                    biting dolls
come on people
            - wake up!
rise to the occasion
please let there be a pulse
  laid within those lax limbs.

two more have just ripened
yes this
        IS how it's done.

bring up the sound
  feel the ground groan
        wasn't there an explosion,
    a demolition of the foundation,
a sense of loss and confusion,
    of groping your way blindly
        knowing there must be a way?

what do you feel
at the base of your shoulders,
            - sensual revelations?

tina
2000

RECONCILIATION

Disparity equates to dumpiness
i think i'll let myself go.
Time borrowed
loaned with interest,
i've built quite a nest
and feathered it with sorrow.

I could melt into the world
put on the air of true age.
Costume it with frumpiness
who would notice?
My heart breaking
facing resignation
consolation of a glorious defeat.

I had true competitants
within this battle
men worthy of my mere mention

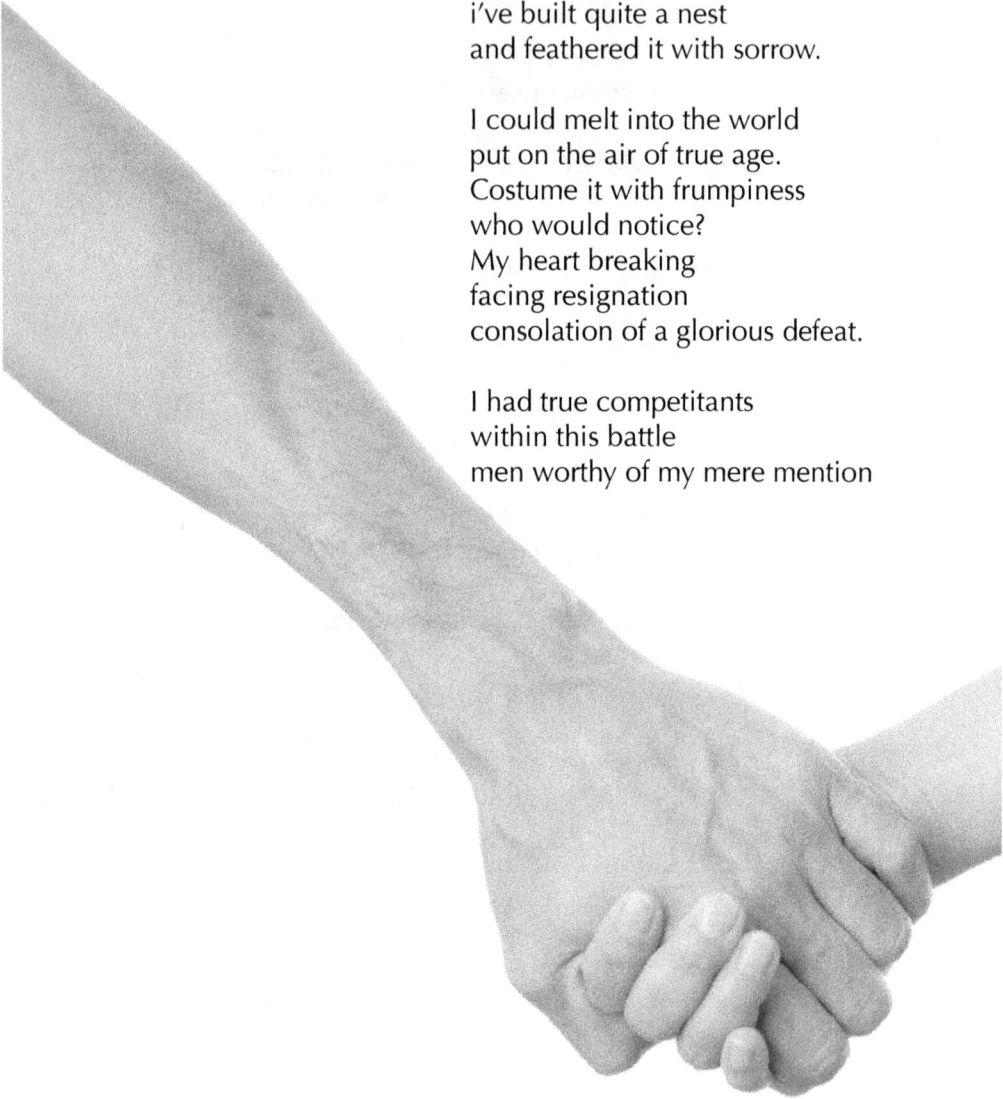

Notoriety noted –

the mountain climber,
the DJ,
the composer pianist,
the giant – twenty years my junior.

the fire-chief,
the dare devil,
the poet,
the gambler I loved so well.

the millionaire,
the queer one,
the systems guru,
the boy who came back a man.

the genius,
the obscene phone caller,
the painter,
the bold young french man.

the dancer,
the physician,
the eagle scout
and finally,
the one who sparked my spirit back in 1966.

Some were the best of friends
Some took ten years before deciding
should I look for another?
Are there any left?

What would I be listed as?
the tarot reader?
the naïve one?

The one who loved them best.

2009
tina

SOLUTION

Hold still please
I promise it won't hurt
it appears much worse than it is

Look I brought some man clues
they're called roses
and chocolates
mostly sweet and red

They're supposed to distract you
long enough

       for you to overlook
       my baggage
       my discrepancies
       my contradicting intentions
       my misconscrewed inflections
       and confusing genuflections

You completely upset my equilibrium
I'm trying to compensate
for my lack of state of mind here

Here, it's out

       Just tell me what you want
           in exchange for
              my crumpled sanity

the offerings are a pittance

       here's my heart as well

       If you would just accept
       my love.

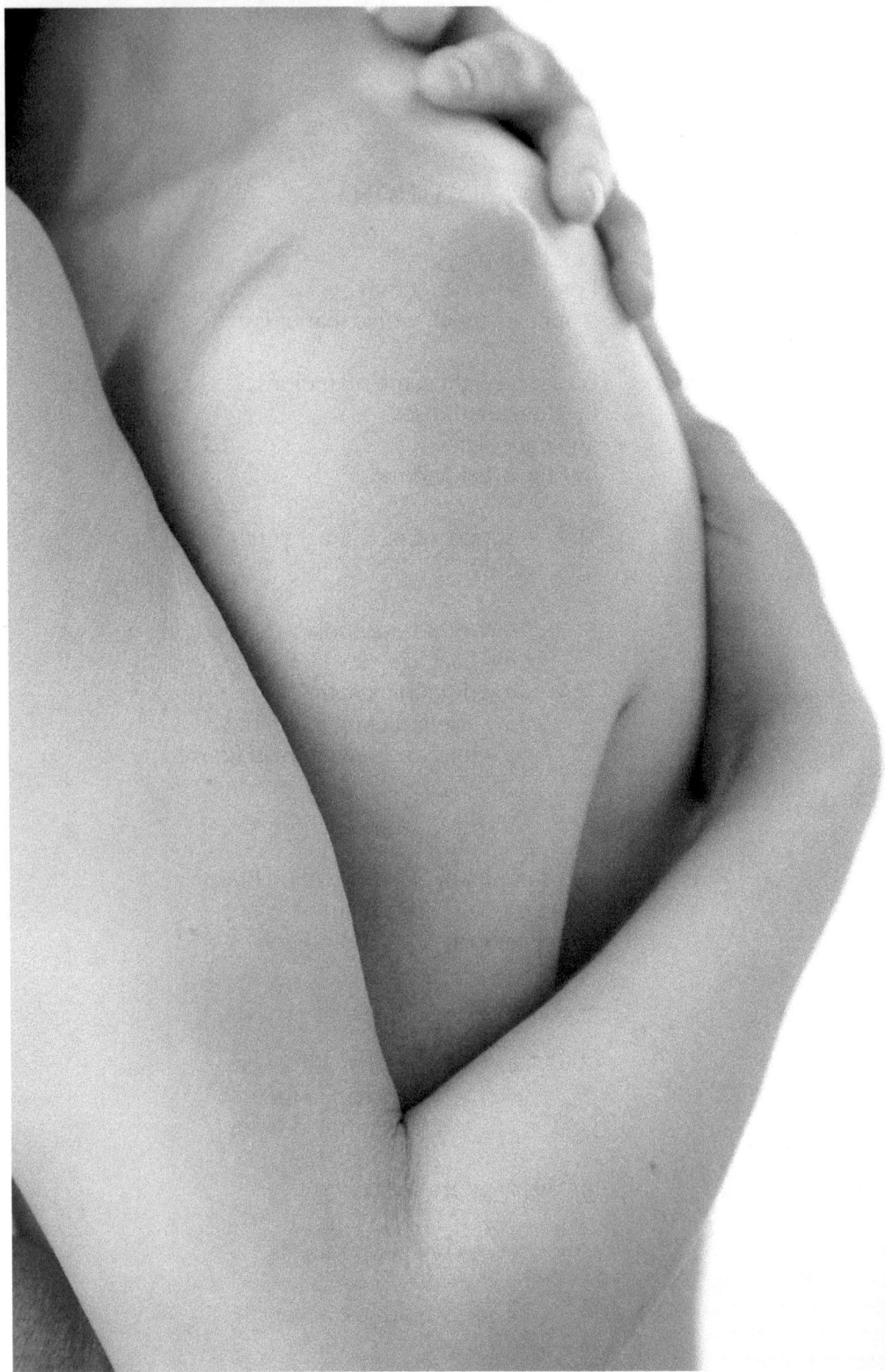

tina
2008

THANK YOU

It's like this
It wasn't love at first sight
It was enchantment at work
a beautiful bird
twittering about on a stage
a resourceful and industrious bird
building that stage himself

Austin, you're a one-man show
I've never seen a bird in a cage
hop upwards from one bar to the next
doing precise one and a half back flips
while playing the sax
yeah, I'm sure you got that 1 2

You are a joy Austin, my Austin
bless you for that
I bless you down on my knees
keep in mind I am a adherent Jew

You give in actions
& in words
protector champion
of the softer gender
irregardless of x y assignment
or choice

You allowed me
my machismo frivolity
and dappered it
with soaked shoulders

Light the beacon
Pulsing Star
Austin, my Austin.

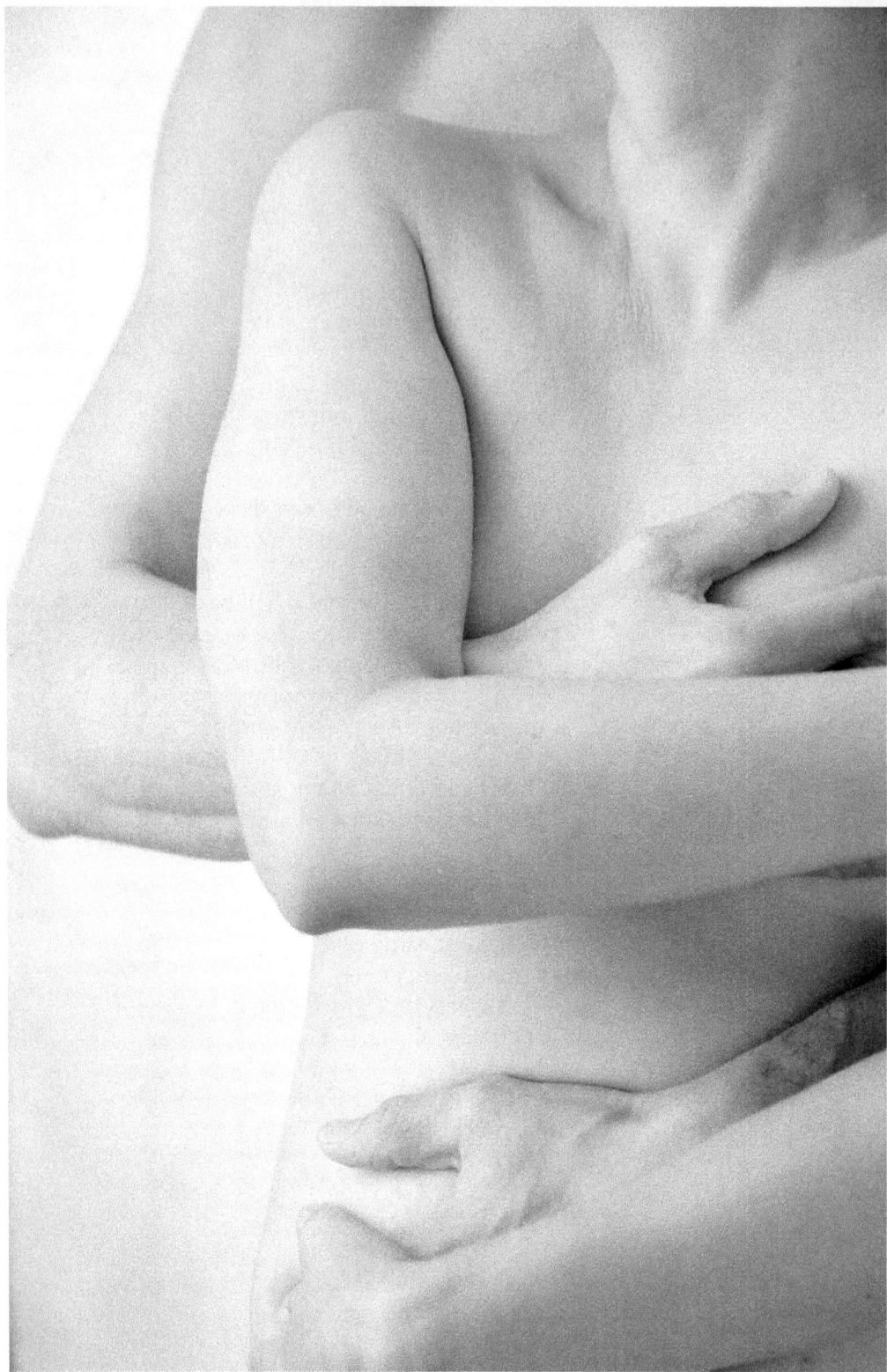

tina
1998

JUST BECAUSE

Just a little darker
just a little firmer
just a little younger

Wishing for another me
the perfect me for you

One not so eager to please
Not afraid to command your presence
your captured attention
a welcomed weakness
to your knees.

Just a little more on top
just a little faster with that shoulder
just a little less self-reliant

Driving me to higher destinations
the perfect me for you

One less hesitant
to casting spells
the breadth
to relieve you of your
troubled discretion

Look - i made you giggle
Squirm a little more
just enough to show
that hope of winter thaw
of a well protected heart.

Just a little closer
just a little less conspicuous
just a little imagination

Bringing you
imperfectuous as you are
to me.

Tina Huerta -- As a movie maker, Tina Huerta has learned to engage film crews and audiences. As a poet she writes, "My venue has always been poetry. That's the place I come from. My poetry is about the grounded moment, the tactile, visceral, sensual element. Sound and touch unite for me so often, maybe I have synesthesia. But being under the skin seems like an excellent place to begin . . . anything. Once you begin, the heart has to open. Open the senses. Open the heart. I've suffered enough for anyone. But I've never stopped returning to my senses."

Anthony V. Auriemma -- We located Anthony again just prior to publication, performing Shakespeare in NYC, where he continues to work conspicuously as an actor. As both a poet and actor, his work has been surfacing repeatedly in the most delicious and surprising places. Because we expect him to both disappear and reappear again, if you happen to spot

him in NYC, let him know that we would love to hear from him! Anthony has performed on stage and film.

Will Turner -- Will is a very composed and precise photographer and videographer currently working in Los Angeles. As photographer for this book, he wanted to produce photographs where the subjects remained untouched. There have been a few minor adjustments to the photographs to account for text overlays, but otherwise Will's photos are just as he intended – unaltered and authentic. Will's work has appeared in over a dozen feature films, and is available to view through willturnerphoto.com.

www.ingramcontent.com/pod-product-compliance
Lightning Source LLC
Chambersburg PA
CBHW060202070426
42447CB00033B/2286

Tina Huerta -- As a movie maker, Tina Huerta has learned to engage film crews and audiences. As a poet she writes, "My venue has always been poetry. That's the place I come from. My poetry is about the grounded moment, the tactile, visceral, sensual element. Sound and touch unite for me so often, maybe I have synesthesia. But being under the skin seems like an excellent place to begin . . . anything. Once you begin, the heart has to open. Open the senses. Open the heart. I've suffered enough for anyone. But I've never stopped returning to my senses."

Anthony V. Auriemma -- We located Anthony again just prior to publication, performing Shakespeare in NYC, where he continues to work conspicuously as an actor. As both a poet and actor, his work has been surfacing repeatedly in the most delicious and surprising places. Because we expect him to both disappear and reappear again, if you happen to spot him in NYC, let him know that we would love to hear from him! Anthony has performed on stage and film.

Will Turner -- Will is a very composed and precise photographer and videographer currently working in Los Angeles. As photographer for this book, he wanted to produce photographs where the subjects remained untouched. There have been a few minor adjustments to the photographs to account for text overlays, but otherwise Will's photos are just as he intended – unaltered and authentic. Will's work has appeared in over a dozen feature films, and is available to view through willturnerphoto.com.

www.ingramcontent.com/pod-product-compliance
Lightning Source LLC
Chambersburg PA
CBHW060202070426
42447CB00033B/2286